T0041834

CONNECTION

CONNECTION

Meditations
& Inspirations

MANDALA

SAN RAFAEL · LOS ANGELES · LONDON

THE PERSON
WHO TRIES
TO LIVE
ALONE
WILL NOT
SUCCEED
AS A HUMAN
BEING.

PEARL S. BUCK

IS THERE
ANYONE
SO WISE AS
TO LEARN
BY THE
EXPERIENCE
OF OTHERS?

VOLTAIRE

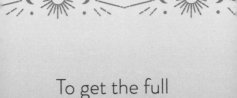

To get the full
value of joy,
you must have
somebody to
divide it with.

MARK TWAIN

We have all known the long loneliness, and we have learned that the only solution is love and that love comes with community.

DOROTHY DAY

ONE WHO
KNOWS HOW
TO SHOW AND
TO ACCEPT
KINDNESS
WILL BE A
FRIEND BETTER
THAN ANY
POSSESSION.

SOPHOCLES

FRIENDSHIP
is based on the
oldest and most
intrinsic human
awareness that
there is more
to life than just
ourselves.

CHRISTOPHER
HANSARD

SHARING
what you have is more
IMPORTANT
than what you have.

ALBERT M. WELLS, JR.

When we
feel love and
kindness
towards others,
it not only
makes others
feel loved and
cared for, but

it helps us also
to develop
inner happiness
and peace.

DALAI LAMA XIV

I KNOW THERE IS **STRENGTH** IN THE DIFFERENCES BETWEEN US. I KNOW THERE IS **COMFORT** WHERE WE OVERLAP.

ANI DIFRANCO

I have begun to
wonder if the
secret of living well
is not in having
all the answers
but in pursuing
unanswerable
questions in good
company.

RACHEL NAOMI REMEN

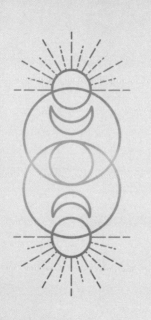

In nature we never see anything isolated, but everything in connection with something else which is before it, beside it, under it, and over it.

JOHANN WOLFGANG
VON GOETHE

Whatever affects one directly, affects all indirectly. For some strange reason, I can never be what I ought to be until you are what you ought to be.

MARTIN LUTHER KING, JR.

If we have no peace, it is because we have forgotten that we belong to each other.

MOTHER TERESA

For a community to be whole and healthy, it must be based on people's love and concern for each other.

MILLARD FULLER

Your destiny is
bound with the
destiny of others.

ANDREW BOYD

Remember, we all stumble, everyone of us. That's why it's a comfort to go hand in hand.

EMILY KIMBROUGH

We do not find the meaning of life by ourselves alone—we find it with another.

THOMAS MERTON

We are never
so defenseless
against suffering
as when we love.

SIGMUND FREUD

EVERYONE NEEDS HELP FROM EVERYONE.

BERTOLT BRECHT

ATTENTION IS VITALITY. IT CONNECTS YOU WITH OTHERS. IT MAKES YOU EAGER. STAY EAGER.

SUSAN SONTAG

There is immense
power when a group
of people with
similar interests
gets together to
work toward the
same goals.

IDOWU KOYENIKAN

IT IS IMPOSSIBLE
TO TRY ONE'S
FRIENDS OUT
IN ADVANCE.

MARCUS TULLIUS
CICERO

The reason it hurts
so much to separate
is because our souls
are connected.

NICHOLAS SPARKS

When watching after yourself, you watch after others. When watching after others, you watch after yourself.

BUDDHA

True friendship
is self-love at
second hand.

WILLIAM HAZLITT

What is a friend? A
single soul dwelling
in two bodies.

ARISTOTLE

I define
connection as
the energy that
exists between
people when they
feel seen, heard,
and valued.

BRENÉ BROWN

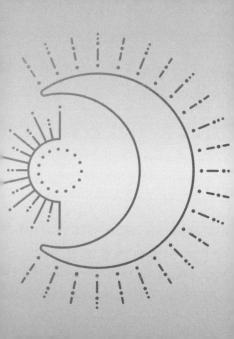

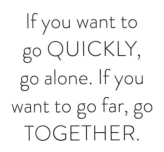

If you want to
go QUICKLY,
go alone. If you
want to go far, go
TOGETHER.

AFRICAN PROVERB

I AM A PART
OF ALL THAT
I HAVE MET.

ALFRED LORD
TENNYSON

You win the

VICTORY

when you yield to

FRIENDS.

SOPHOCLES

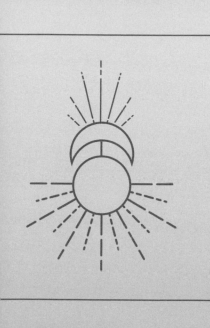

THE TRUE
MEANING OF
LIFE IS TO PLANT
TREES UNDER
WHOSE SHADE
YOU DO NOT
EXPECT TO SIT.

NELSON HENDERSON

Good company
and good discourse
are the very
sinews of virtue.

IZAAK WALTON

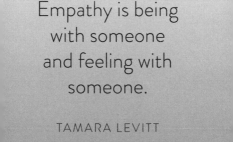

Empathy is being
with someone
and feeling with
someone.

TAMARA LEVITT

The most
EXQUISITE
pleasure is giving
PLEASURE
to others.

JEAN DE LA BRUYÈRE

LIVE SO
THAT YOUR
FRIENDS
CAN DEFEND
YOU BUT
NEVER
HAVE TO.

ARNOLD H.
GLASGOW

The golden way is to be friends with the world and to regard the whole human family as one.

MAHATMA GANDHI

THE WORST
SOLITUDE IS TO
BE DESTITUTE
OF SINCERE
FRIENDSHIP.

FRANCIS BACON

Real unselfishness
comes in sharing
the interests
of others.

GEORGE SANTAYANA

TO LIVE IS NOT
TO LIVE FOR
ONE'S SELF
ALONE; LET
US HELP ONE
ANOTHER.

MENANDER

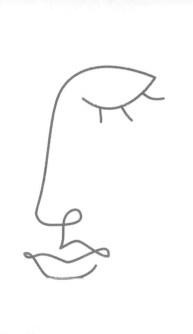

You can no more
separate one life
from another
than you can
separate a breeze
from the wind.

MITCH ALBOM

Where there is great love, there are always miracles.

WILLA CATHER

If you want to
be listened to,
you should put in
time listening.

MARGE PIERCY

The more complex
the network is,
the more complex
its pattern of
interconnections,
the more resilient
it will be.

FRITJOF CAPRA

The minute
we become an
integrated whole,
we look through
the same eyes
and we see a
whole different
world together.

AZIZAH AL-HIBRI

Habituated patterns
create distance...
openness and
truth bring us
closer together.

CHARLOTTE KASL

To give service
to a single heart
by a single act
is better than a
thousand heads
bowing in prayer.

MAHATMA GANDHI

They may forget what you said, but they will never forget how you made them feel.

CARL W. BUEHNER

It is one of the
most beautiful
compensations
of this life that
no man can
sincerely try to help
another without
helping himself.

RALPH WALDO
EMERSON

One can bear
grief, but it takes
two to be glad.

ELBERT HUBBARD

OUR
AFFECTIONS
ARE OUR LIFE.
WE LIVE BY
THEM; THEY
SUPPLY OUR
WARMTH.

WILLIAM ELLERY
CHANNING

Love lights more fires than hate extinguishes.

ELLA WHEELER WILCOX

We are all connected—
to each other,
biologically; to the
earth, chemically;
to the rest of the
universe, atomically.

NEIL DEGRASSE TYSON

If you JUDGE
people, you
have no time to
LOVE them.

MOTHER TERESA

AGE DOES NOT
PROTECT YOU
FROM LOVE,
BUT LOVE, TO
SOME EXTENT,
PROTECTS YOU
FROM AGE.

JEANNE MOREAU

We cannot live
only for ourselves.

HERMAN MELVILLE

WE CANNOT
HOLD A TORCH
TO LIGHT
ANOTHER'S
PATH WITHOUT
BRIGHTENING
OUR OWN.

BEN SWEETLAND

I LOVE, AND THE WORLD IS MINE!

FLORENCE EARLE
COATES

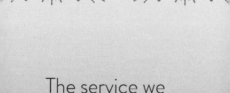

The service we render others is the rent we pay for our room on earth.

WILFRED GRENFELL

EVERYTHING
THAT LIVES,
LIVES NOT
ALONE, NOR
FOR ITSELF.

WILLIAM BLAKE

Real friendship
is shown in times
of trouble.

EURIPIDES

Affinities are rare.
They come but a
few times in a life. It
is awful to risk losing
one when it arrives.

FLORENCE H.
WINTERBURN

The gift of paying
attention is a
fundamental key
to transforming
our relationships.

DEEPAK CHOPRA

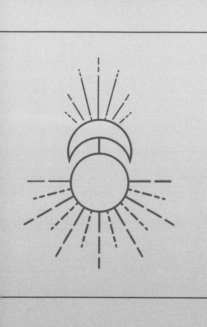

A bit of fragrance
always clings to
the hand that
gives you roses.

CHINESE PROVERB

We are like islands
in the sea, separate
on the surface
but connected
in the deep.

WILLIAM JAMES

I believe that every human mind feels pleasure in doing good to another.

THOMAS JEFFERSON

If you understand,
and you show that
you understand,
you can love,
and the situation
will change.

THÍCH NHẤT HẠNH

We are members,
one of another, so
that you cannot
injure or help
your neighbor
without injuring or
helping yourself.

GEORGE BERNARD
SHAW

NO ROAD IS LONG WITH GOOD COMPANY.

TURKISH PROVERB

Treat everyone
you meet as if
they were you.

DOUG DILLON

The greatness of a community is most accurately measured by the compassionate actions of its members.

CORETTA SCOTT KING

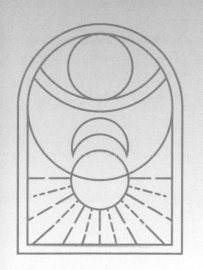

Life is partly what
we make it and
partly what is made
by the friends
we choose.

TENNESSEE WILLIAMS

The entire
population of the
universe, with one
trifling exception,
is composed
of others.

JOHN ANDREW HOLMES

It is enough that
I am of value to
somebody today.

HUGH PRATHER

Never doubt that
a small group
of thoughtful,
committed citizens
can change the
world; indeed,
it's the only thing
that ever has.

MARGARET MEAD

THERE IS
NOTHING ON
THIS EARTH
MORE TO
BE PRIZED
THAN TRUE
FRIENDSHIP.

SAINT THOMAS AQUINAS

Hold a true
friend with both
your hands.

NIGERIAN PROVERB

Good communication is as stimulating as black coffee, and just as hard to sleep after.

ANNE MORROW
LINDBERGH

PLEASURE IS
A NECESSARY
RECIPROCAL.
NO ONE FEELS
WHO DOES NOT
AT THE SAME
TIME GIVE IT.

LORD CHESTERFIELD

The fate of this man
or that man was
less than a drop,
although it was a
sparkling one, in the
great blue motion
of the sunlit sea.

T.H. WHITE

No man can be happy without a friend, nor be sure of his friend until he is unhappy.

THOMAS FULLER

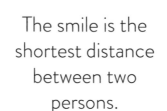

The smile is the
shortest distance
between two
persons.

VICTOR BORGE

A man wrapped up
in himself makes a
very small bundle.

BENJAMIN FRANKLIN

One of the deep secrets of life is that all that is really worth doing is what we do for others.

LEWIS CARROLL

I cannot concentrate all my friendship on any single one of my friends because no one is complete enough in himself.

ANAÏS NIN

You don't get
HARMONY
when everyone
sings the same
NOTE.

DOUG FLOYD

To be capable of
steady friendship
or lasting love are
the two greatest
proofs, not only
of goodness
of heart but of
strength of mind.

WILLIAM HAZLITT

No man is an island,
entire of itself
every man is a piece
of the continent, a
part of the main.

JOHN DONNE

The best way to
find out if you can
trust somebody
is to trust them.

ERNEST HEMINGWAY

GENEROSITY
gives assistance
rather than
ADVICE.

MARQUIS DE
VAUVENARGUES

LOVE IS THE
ONLY THING
WE CAN CARRY
WITH US WHEN
WE GO, AND
IT MAKES THE
END SO EASY.

LOUISA MAY ALCOTT

I alone cannot change the world, but I can cast a stone across the waters to create many ripples.

MOTHER TERESA

PROVISION
for others is a
FUNDAMENTAL
responsibility of
HUMAN LIFE.

WOODROW WILSON

When you
cease to make a
contribution, you
begin to die.

ELEANOR ROOSEVELT

THE BEAUTY
YOU SEE
IN ME IS A
REFLECTION
OF YOU.

RUMI

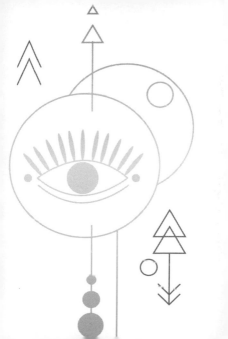

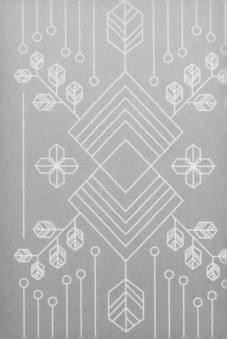

A DREAM
YOU DREAM
ALONE IS ONLY
A DREAM.
A DREAM
YOU DREAM
TOGETHER
IS REALITY.

YOKO ONO

The entire sum of
existence is the
magic of being
needed by just
one person.

VII PUTNAM

BE KIND
WHENEVER
POSSIBLE.
IT IS ALWAYS
POSSIBLE.

DALAI LAMA XIV

One of the most important things you can do on this earth is to let people know they are not alone.

SHANNON L. ALDER

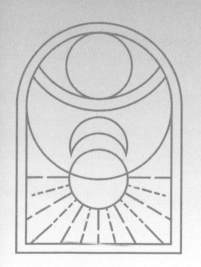

Kindness can become its own motive. We are made kind by being kind.

ERIC HOFFER

Happiness never decreases by being shared.

BUKKYO DENDO KYOKAI

Wear a smile and
have friends;
wear a scowl and
have wrinkles.

GEORGE ELIOT

What can you do
to promote world
peace? Go home
and love your family.

MOTHER TERESA

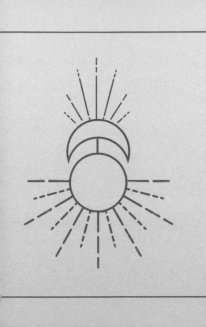

Community, above all, is bigger than individuals; we are something much more than individuals when we are part of a community.

TONY BLACKSHAW

THE MEASURE
OF LOVE IS TO
LOVE WITHOUT
MEASURE.

SAINT FRANCIS
DE SALES

Even the
technology that
promises to unite
us divides us.

DAN BROWN

ALL WHO JOY
WOULD WIN
MUST SHARE IT—
HAPPINESS WAS
BORN A TWIN.

LORD BYRON

WE WERE BORN
TO UNITE WITH
OUR FELLOW
MEN AND
TO JOIN IN
COMMUNITY
WITH THE
HUMAN RACE.

MARCUS TULLIUS
CICERO

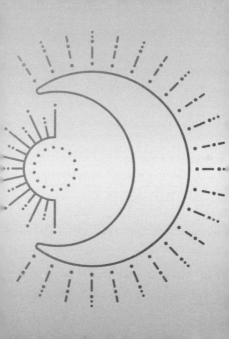

We all live with the objective of being happy; our lives are all different, and yet the same.

ANNE FRANK

A good friend is my nearest relation.

THOMAS FULLER

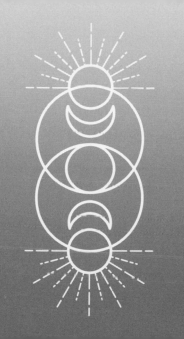

The more we
genuinely care
about others, the
greater our own
happiness and
inner peace.

ALLAN LOKOS

FORGIVING
THOSE WHO
HURT US IS
THE KEY TO
PERSONAL
PEACE.

ULYSSES G. WEATHERLY

When we get too caught up in the busyness of the world, we lose connection with one another—and ourselves.

JACK KORNFIELD

Love and compassion are necessities, not luxuries. Without them humanity cannot survive.

DALAI LAMA XIV

LOVE cannot
live where there
is no TRUST.

EDITH HAMILTON

COMPASSION
IS THE BASIS OF
ALL MORALITY.

ARTHUR SCHOPENHAUER

Every person is
defined by the
communities she
belongs to.

ORSON SCOTT CARD

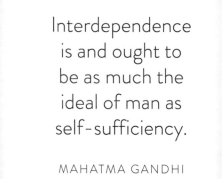

Interdependence is and ought to be as much the ideal of man as self-sufficiency.

MAHATMA GANDHI

HAVE FRIENDS.
'TIS A SECOND
EXISTENCE.

BALTASAR GRACIÁN

YOU CANNOT
BE LONELY
IF YOU LIKE
THE PERSON
YOU ARE
ALONE WITH.

WAYNE DYER

The supreme
happiness of life
is the conviction
that we are loved.

VICTOR HUGO

SINCE YOU
CANNOT DO
GOOD TO ALL,
YOU ARE TO
PAY SPECIAL
ATTENTION TO
THOSE WHO, BY
THE ACCIDENTS
OF TIME, OR
PLACE, OR

CIRCUMSTANCES, ARE BROUGHT INTO CLOSER CONNECTION WITH YOU.

AUGUSTINE OF HIPPO

He that walketh
with wise men
shall be wise.

SOLOMON

Only a life lived
for others is a
life worthwhile.

ALBERT EINSTEIN

HELP YOUR
BROTHER'S
BOAT ACROSS
AND YOUR
OWN WILL
REACH THE
SHORE.

HINDU PROVERB

Eventually
everything
connects—people,
ideas, objects.
The quality of the
connections is the
key to quality per se.

CHARLES EAMES

INSTINCT
TEACHES US
TO LOOK FOR
HAPPINESS
OUTSIDE
OURSELVES.

BLAISE PASCAL

If we had no regard for others' feelings or fortune, we would grow cold and indifferent to life itself.

GEORGE MATTHEW ADAMS

ALONE, WE
CAN DO
SO LITTLE;
TOGETHER,
WE CAN DO
SO MUCH.

HELEN KELLER

Adversity not
only draws people
together but brings
forth that beautiful
inward friendship.

SØREN KIERKEGAARD

The true way
to soften one's
troubles is to
solace those
of others.

MADAME DE
MAINTENON

BE BRAVE
ENOUGH
TO ACCEPT
THE HELP OF
OTHERS.

MELBA COLGROVE

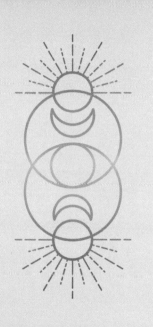

Set your life
on fire. Seek
those who fan
your flames.

RUMI

TO BE
SOCIAL
IS TO BE
FORGIVING.

ROBERT FROST

Friendship improves
happiness and
abates misery, by
the doubling of
our joy and the
dividing of our grief.

MARCUS TULLIUS
CICERO

ONE'S FRIENDS
ARE THAT
PART OF THE
HUMAN RACE
WITH WHICH
ONE CAN BE
HUMAN.

GEORGE SANTAYANA

THERE IS NO
HOPE OR
JOY EXCEPT
IN HUMAN
RELATIONS.

ANTOINE DE
SAINT-EXUPÉRY

INVISIBLE
threads are the
strongest ties.

FRIEDRICH
NIETZSCHE

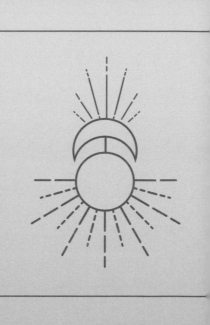

HEALING
yourself is
connected
with healing
OTHERS.

YOKO ONO

The habit of being uniformly considerate toward others will bring increased happiness to you.

GRENVILLE KLEISER

Society is no
COMFORT
to one not
sociable.

WILLIAM SHAKESPEARE

THE BEST
TIME TO MAKE
FRIENDS IS
BEFORE YOU
NEED THEM.

ETHEL BARRYMORE

We all of us need assistance. Those who sustain others themselves want to be sustained.

MAURICE D'HULST

Communication is merely an exchange of information, but connection is an exchange of our humanity.

SEAN STEPHENSON

'Tis the privilege of friendship to talk nonsense and have her nonsense respected.

CHARLES LAMB

When we try to
pick out anything
by itself, we find
it hitched to
everything else
in the Universe.

JOHN MUIR

People seldom improve when they have no other model but themselves to copy after.

OLIVER GOLDSMITH

A FRIEND
MAY WELL BE
RECKONED THE
MASTERPIECE
OF NATURE.

RALPH WALDO
EMERSON

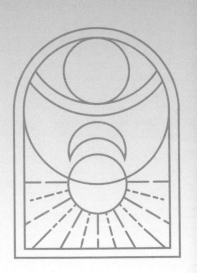

Intimacy requires courage because risk is inescapable.

ROLLO MAY

NO BIRD SOARS
TOO HIGH IF HE
SOARS WITH HIS
OWN WINGS.

WILLIAM BLAKE

CONVERSATION
is the most human and
HUMANIZING
thing we do.

SHERRY TURKLE

MANDALA

P.O. Box 3088
San Rafael, CA 94912
www.MandalaEarth.com

CEO: Raoul Goff
Editorial Director: Katie Killebrew
VP Creative: Chrissy Kwasnik
VP Manufacturing: Alix Nicholaeff
Associate Art Director: Ashley Quackenbush
Designer: Amy DeGrote
Project Editor: Claire Yee
Production Manager: Andy Harper

978-1-64722-579-7
Manufactured in China by Insight Editions
10 9 8 7 6 5 4 3 2 1
2022 2023 2024